Contents

Get the basics

Plain pencils and dull book covers are just fine, but why not add some fun to your everyday school items? With a few materials, you can turn your school supplies into one-of-a-kind works of art.

If you don't have exactly what you need for each project, you can often improvise. For example, if you don't have an old pair of jeans for the pocket book cover, try an old shirt with a pocket instead. Be creative!

WARNING

On pages where you see this symbol, ask an adult for help.

ROCK YOUR SCHOOL LIFE

...orres

QED

QED Publishing

Copyright © QED Publishing 2010

First published in the UK in 2010 by
QED Publishing
A Quarto Group company
226 City Road
London EC1V 2TT
www.qed-publishing.co.uk

A catalogue record for this book is available
from the British Library.

ISBN 978 1 84835 453 1

Printed in China

Editor: Eve Marleau
Designer: Lisa Peacock
Photographer: Simon Pask
Project Maker: Sue Hunter-Jones

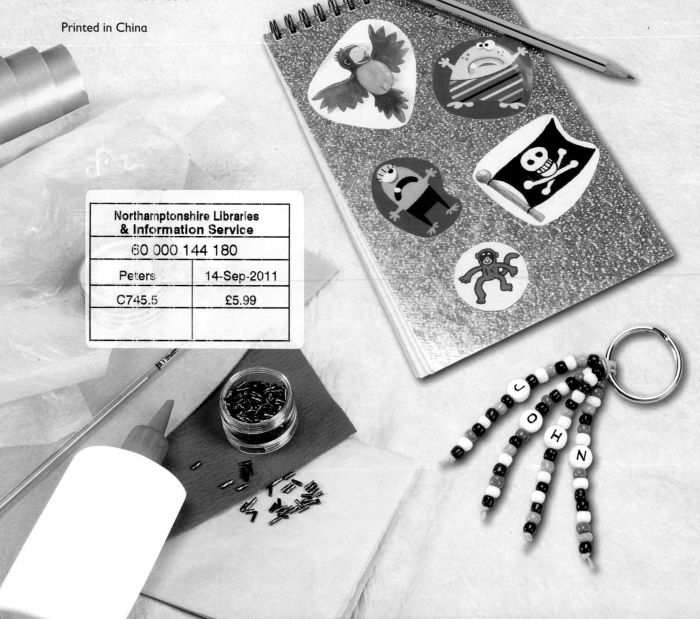

Here are a few of the basic craft items you will need for some of the projects:

Glitter - Any kind of glitter works with the projects in this book, from fine to chunky. You can even use tiny beads or microbeads instead.

Scissors - Make sure you always have a good pair of scissors for cutting materials such as paper, felt and wool in the projects.

Embroidery thread - Embroidery thread is made up of six or more threads per strand. It also comes as a single, thick strand.

Glue - If a project calls for 'glue' you can use whatever you might have around the house. 'White glue' means a white standard glue. 'Craft glue' means a thick white glue that won't run or spread.

Always remember...
When making a project, protect the surface you are working on with newspaper or plastic for a mess-free, easy clean-up.

Fuzzy pencil toppers

Add a little fun to your pens and pencils with these fuzzy, bouncy toppers.

YOU WILL NEED
- Pen or pencil
- Pipe cleaners
- Glue
- Googly eyes

Step 1

Hold the pipe cleaner against the middle of the pencil at a 90-degree angle with your thumb.

Step 2

Coil the pipe cleaner tightly around the pencil, one coil right next to the other.

Step 3

Push the coil up the pencil so that about two-thirds of it is off the end of the pencil.

Use two different-coloured pipe cleaners for a fun effect.

Step 4

Hold on to the coils still on the pencil and pull on the other end of the pipe cleaner just enough to make the coils look like a spring.

Step 5

Use the glue to stick googly eyes to the end of the pipe cleaner.

Customized stickers

You can turn any paper designs into stickers. Use them to decorate your school papers, notebooks or folders.

YOU WILL NEED

- 1 tablespoon of white vinegar
- 2 tablespoons of white glue
- Measuring spoons
- Paper cup
- Plastic spoon
- Paintbrush
- Paper images
- Scissors
- Sponge or cloth

Step 1

Cut images from scraps of wrapping paper, magazines or any other material you can find.

Step 2

Put the vinegar and glue in the cup. Mix them together with the plastic spoon.

8

Step 3

Using the paintbrush, spread an even, thin coat of the mixture on the back of the paper. Let dry.

Add some sparkle to your stickers with glitter.

Step 4

Use a damp sponge or cloth to moisten the stickers when you're ready to stick them.

Step 5

Use the stickers to decorate your school notebooks.

Backpack zip pulls

Customize your backpack with these cool zip pulls. You'll never lose your bag in the changing rooms!

Step 1

Attach the string to the keyring by threading it through and pulling the ends through to form a loop.

Step 2

Attach several pieces of string, then thread pony beads onto them.

Step 3

Thread the alphabet beads onto one of the strings to spell your name.

Step 4

Tie knots at the end of each string to secure the beads.

Step 5

Attach the keyring to the zip on your backpack.

Use the colours of your school sports team on a pull for your gym bag.

Taped-up notebook

Have the coolest notebook in class with this unique duct tape cover.

YOU WILL NEED

- Duct tape (at least two colours)
- Notebook
- Waxed or parchment paper
- Pen or marker
- Scissors

Step 1

Cover the notebook by sticking on strips of duct tape. Make sure the strips overlap each other slightly.

Step 2

Cut the strips a little longer than the notebook cover and fold them over the edges at the top and bottom.

Step 3

Stick a few pieces of duct tape in a different colour on the waxed or parchment paper.

Step 4

Draw shapes on the back side of the duct tape on the paper. A ball point pen or permanent marker works best. Cut out the shapes.

Step 5

Remove the waxed paper or parchment paper and stick the duct tape shapes onto the notebook.

Why not add some fun stickers to give your notebook a bright touch?

Beaded pens

Bring on the bling with these cool beaded pens. Your pencil case will look like it belongs to a rock star!

Step 1

Cut a piece of tape as long as the barrel of the pen. Stick the tape to the pen barrel. Remove the backing.

Step 2

Cut another piece of tape and stick it to the other side of the pen barrel. Make sure the edges of the tape overlap.

Try co-ordinating the colour of your beads with the pen.

Step 3

Pour the beads into the tray. Roll the pen around in the beads so most of the pen is covered. Remove any leftover beads from the tray.

Step 4

Hold the pen over the tray and pour glitter over it. The glitter will fill in the spaces between the beads.

People pencil toppers

Create a bunch of pencil pals to keep you company while you're doing homework.

↑
Once you have made the pencil topper, cut the hair spiky for a punky look!

Step 1

Cut about 10 strands of thread about 7 centimetres long to make the hair. Bend a pipe cleaner in half over the middle of the thread.

Step 2

Thread the ends of the pipe cleaner through the bead so the hair sticks out of the top of the bead.

Step 3

Twist the ends of the pipe cleaner around the pencil. Let the ends of the pipe cleaner stick out at the sides for arms.

Step 4

Twist the second pipe cleaner around the pencil, underneath the arms.

Step 5

Draw eyes on the bead with a pen.

Sweet-tin stationery box

This is a handy container that you can easily keep in your backpack for paper clips, rubber bands, coins and other small items.

 You can use your box to store keepsakes, too.

Step 1

Wash and dry the sweet tin.

Step 2

Cut out enough paper images to cover the top of the box.

Step 3

Mix 1 tablespoon of white glue with 1 tablespoon of water in a paper cup. Paint a layer of the mixture over the top of the box.

Step 4

Stick down the images in the glue mixture. Overlap them so the whole tin top is covered.

Step 5

Paint another layer of glue over the images and let dry. Cut a piece of coloured paper to fit in the bottom of the tin and place inside.

Jumbo clip bookmark

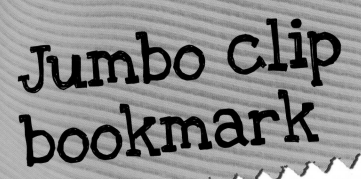

These giant bookmarks will hold your place in style, and won't slide out of the book.

➡ Try making these bookmarks as fun gifts for friends.

Step 1

Cut the cord or ribbon to about 50 centimetres long.

Step 2

Thread the cord or ribbon through the paper clip on one side, then thread the other end through on the opposite side.

Step 3

Pull both ends of the cord or ribbon through the paper clip to secure.

Step 4

Glue some buttons on the ends of the ribbon. Let dry.

Step 5

Clip your bookmark onto a page in your book.

Graffiti book covers

YOU WILL NEED
- Brown paper
- Pencil
- Coloured pencils
- Scissors

Protect your books and express your own style with custom book covers. You can use any kind of heavy-duty paper such as wrapping paper or brown paper.

Step 1

Lay the brown paper out flat on a table, wrong side up. Open the book and place it on the paper.

↑ Try drawing bright fish and flowers on your summer term notebook.

Step 2

Cut the brown paper around the book so there is 5 centimetres extra at the top and bottom and about 12 centimetres along the sides.

Step 3

Make a pencil mark on the brown paper at the top and bottom edges. Remove the book and fold the paper at the marks.

Step 4

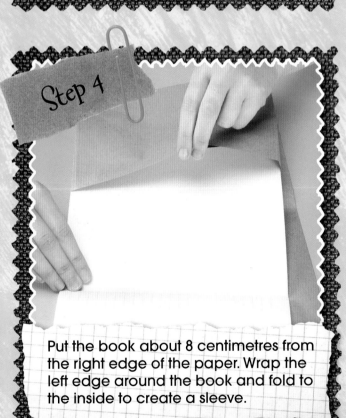

Put the book about 8 centimetres from the right edge of the paper. Wrap the left edge around the book and fold to the inside to create a sleeve.

Step 5

Open the cover of the book and slide the paper sleeve over the cover. Cover the paper in graffiti-style designs.

Pocket book cover

Use a pocket from an old pair of trousers to make a pocket on a notebook to hold pens, pencils and erasers.

Try adding buttons to brighten up a denim cover.

Step 1

Cut off a leg of the trousers. Trace around the cover of the book on the thigh part of the trousers.

Step 2

Glue the fabric to the notebook. Let dry.

Step 3

Cut out a pocket from the trousers. Make sure you cut around the whole thing so the fabric on the back of the pocket stays on.

Step 4

Slip a piece of waxed paper in the pocket. Spread glue all over the back of the pocket. Press onto the front of the binder. Let dry.

Step 5

When the glue is dry, remove the waxed paper. You can add stickers to customize the pocket.

25

Mini-notepads

These mini-notepads are perfectly pocket size. You can make notes in them, or tear pages out when you need to pass something along to a friend.

YOU WILL NEED
- Card
- Paper
- Scissors
- Ruler
- Stapler
- Paper images (for decoration)

Step 1

Cut a piece of card 7 x 21 centimetres. With the wrong side up, fold up the bottom edge by 2.5 centimetres. Fold up one more time.

Step 2

Fold the opposite end down, so the edge is in the middle of the fold.

Step 3

Cut 12 or more pieces of paper to 6 x 7 centimetres.

Step 4

Stack the papers and place them inside the fold. Staple them in place, about 1 centimetre up from the bottom. Tuck in the front cover.

Step 5

Glue an image to the front of your notepad to decorate.

Try drawing your own image and sticking it to the notepad.

Sweet treat pencil holder

Use recycled sweet wrappers to make this container for your pens and pencils.

YOU WILL NEED

- Sweet wrappers
- Glue
- Empty juice carton
- Clear sticky tape
- Felt or cardboard
- Scissors

Step 1

Clean out the empty juice carton and dry thoroughly. Cut the top off the carton.

Step 2

Glue the sweet wrappers on the carton, overlapping edges so the whole carton is covered. Let dry completely.

Step 3

Use strips of tape to stick the sweet wrappers around the carton.

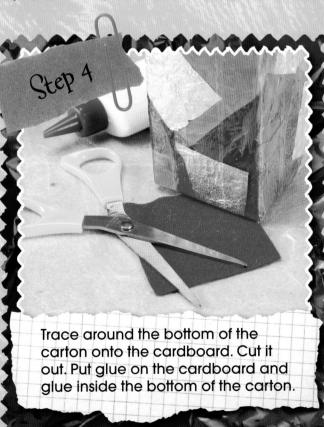

Step 4

Trace around the bottom of the carton onto the cardboard. Cut it out. Put glue on the cardboard and glue inside the bottom of the carton.

Try using lots of different sweet wrappers for a brighter look.

29

Rock a recycled style

You can use recycled materials from around the house to make some of the projects. Here are a few ideas.

Page 8

Customized stickers

Keep your eyes out for images on paper that you can recycle into stickers. Wrapping paper, magazine pages and scrap paper are a few places to look.

Page 12

Taped-up notebook

If you have an old notebook, you can rip out the used pages. It doesn't matter what's on the cover, because it will be covered in tape.

Page 18

Sweet-tin stationery box

Cut stamps from envelopes that have come to your house in the post to decorate your sweet tin.

Index